LOONY LIMERICKS

FROM THE

MIKE FLYNN SHOW
BBC RADIO WALES

£1.50
Purchase of this copy ensures a donation of 20p to the Detective Constable Alun Williams Fund.

THE STARLING PRESS LTD
PUBLISHERS & PRINTERS
RISCA NEWPORT GWENT
GREAT BRITAIN
1983

Introduction:

F E A YATES, Publisher-in-Chief, Starling Press Ltd

Mike Flynn invited me to BBC Llandaff to discuss the publication of this volume of Limericks. Our forte is in producing, by South Wales writers, Local History titles of the towns and villages of South Wales. He reminded me that the majority of contributors were residents in South Wales, and could be included as South Wales authors! When he spoke of 10,000 verses, I was drained of enthusiasm. The cost of production terrified me. The final decision to publish 5000 copies, each with 420 verses is one of a gambler. I hope sales continue so that we can offer the target figure of £1000 to the Detective Constable Alan Williams Fund.

First Edition 1983

© Contributors & BBC Radio Wales

ISBN 0 903434 65 2

Printed by The Starling Press Ltd, Risca, Newport, Gwent NP1 6YB
Finishing by Geo Tremewan & Son, Swansea

MIKE FLYNN

MIKE FLYNN: Presenter, BBC Radio Wales

I never thought **LOONY LIMERICKS** would play such a prominent part in my daily programme on BBC Radio Wales when I introduced the idea about three years ago.

From the start they were a resounding success: so much so that the **LIMERICK COMPETITION** is now as much a part of the show as I am.

This lighthearted feature, originally planned to run for a few months, has brought me and the staff in the BBC office endless hours of mirth.

It has also prompted regular correspondence from people in all walks of life, from nine years old to ninety years old, from listeners living in the Principality and beyond.

Literally hundreds of these amusing little rhymes reach my desk at Broadcasting House, Cardiff every week. The Loony Limerick Challenge has been taken up in some unusual quarters: people get hooked on them very easily it seems.

DENNIS COLLINS, the cartoonist, who draws the **DAILY MIRROR'S** long running **'PERISHERS'** cartoon strip, is a name you will see popping up in these pages. I even thought about including the lady who pleads in a postscript "Please Mike don't mention my name, as I don't want the neighbours to know!"

From Day One I made a point of keeping all the limericks sent to me. This book contains just a small collection from more than 10,000 contributions sent before spring of 1982. My problem has always been, both in the programme and this book, to decide which to include and which to omit. I'm glad that I didn't have to make that decision on my own!!

This book is dedicated to all my **LOONY LIMERICK** writers. My thanks to everyone who, at some time has put pen to paper to share a smile with others.

I hope you enjoy this book.

3

Thanks to all contributors
IN APPRECIATION:

My special thanks to the following without whose efforts these limericks would still be in dozens of brown envelopes inside a BBC filing cabinet.

ALAN BADMINGTON: Took on the task of sifting through the limericks. I found his expertise as a judge invaluable. You question his ability? Let me tell you that since first entering my competition a few years ago he has won in other competitions more than £8,500 worth of prizes for limerick writing. (Thankfully, just £5 was from Radio Wales!!) Alan is a Sergeant with the Gwent Constabulary, based at Pontypool.

KEN KING: Responsible for the marvellous cartoons in this book: also employed by the Gwent Constabulary: studied art and has contributed to a number of magazines: lives in Rogerstone, Gwent.

PIET BRINTON: Provided the cover cartoon: a colleague of mine at BBC Radio Wales. An excellent artist and graphic designer, also a good broadcaster, songwriter, musician, carpenter, plumber and wit! I've yet to find something he can't do! Luckily he lives in Saundersfoot, which is too far from Cardiff, to want my job.

SPECIAL THANKS also to BBC Radio Wales; BBC Publications; **PETER TREMEWAN** (Bookbinder in Swansea); Postmen everywhere for identifying some of the more 'offbeat' addressed letters for delivery to the Mike Flynn Office; Programme Secretary Val Handley for coping with me, all those phone calls, the Tea Lady and the mail (usually all at the same time!).

Thank you to **F E A YATES OF STARLING PRESS OF RISCA** whose sterling efforts as a Publisher put this volume into print. Alan said 'yes' when other Publishers said 'No' and his enthusiasm has overwhelmed me.

Two Officers from the Gwent Police Force have contributed a great deal to this effort. Royalties of 20p each book are being donated to the fund to help Detective Constable Alan Williams of the Gwent Constabulary who lost his sight in a shooting incident while carrying out his duties during 1982.

F E A YATES

PETER TREMEWAN

THE MAYOR OF A LITTLE WELSH TOWN

The mayor of a little Welsh town
Said "At luncheons I feel such a clown
My chain tends to droop
And dips in the soup
Whenever I try to sit down".

> Cath and Eric Gauron
> Radyr, Cardiff, South Glam.

The mayor of a little Welsh town
Was noted for swigging it down
To pay for his scotch
He pawned his best watch
And his chain for some bottles of brown.

> W. J. Delve
> West Cross, Swansea, West Glam.

A mayor of a little Welsh town
Says tourists don't cause him a frown
When Eastern ones call
He meets them in the hall
Wearing turban and red dressing gown.

> M. Lusty
> Newport, Gwent

A mayor of a little Welsh town
Said "Visit us here to get brown
It's not the sun, man
Which gives us a tan
But rust from the rain that pours down".

> Jean Oriel
> Mountain Ash, Mid Glam.

A DRIVING INSTRUCTOR FROM GWENT

A driving instructor from Gwent
Was known as a God fearing gent
He was once known to pray
Through the whole month of May
'Cos he knelt in quick drying cement.

> Harry Hartill
> Rhydyfelin, Pontypridd, Mid Glam.

A driving instructor from Gwent
Used much stronger fuel than he meant
While giving tuition
Switched on the ignition
And up into orbit he went.

> W. J. Delve
> West Cross, Swansea, West Glam.

A driving instructor from Gwent
Said "Left on the bridge, please Miss Kent
Don't take it too tight"
But the lady turned right
And into the river they went.

> Brian E. Wood
> Creigiau, Nr. Cardiff, South Glam.

A driving instructor from Gwent
Said "A new highway code I'll invent
For my pupils are fools
They break all the rules
As up 'One Way' streets, I am sent".

> Coral Courtney,
> Llanelli, Dyfed

A SWEEPER WHO JOINED SWANSEA TOWN

A sweeper who joined Swansea Town
Turned the rules of the game upside down
If he scored, you can bet
It was in his own net
His transfer fee's now half-a-crown.

> Bob Wolfson
> Cardiff, South Glam.

A sweeper who joined Swansea Town
For his drinking prowess was renown
Before every match
He would sink down the hatch
Six whiskies, five gins and a brown.

> Alan Badmington
> Abergavenny, Gwent

A sweeper who joined Swansea Town
Was called Rupert Fortesque Brown
Though his name sounded posh
He did not impress Tosh
For his shots hit the corner flags down.

> W. J. Delve
> West Cross, Swansea, West Glam.

A sweeper who joined Swansea Town
Pranced around like a scarlet-nosed clown
But his knicker elastic
Was not too fantastic
Like his coupon, his drawers let him down.

> Jean Griffiths
> Mountain Ash, Mid Glam.

A BURGLAR WHO BURGLED A BANK

A burglar who burgled a bank
Was as thick as a carpenter's plank
He carried a bag
Which was plainly marked 'Swag'
And the shells in his gun were all blank.

> W. J. Delve
> Swansea, West Glam.

A burglar who burgled a bank
Is known to all as a crank
Despite all he stole
He still draws his dole
In a Rolls, with a solid gold tank.

> Bob Wolfson
> Cardiff, South Glam.

A burglar who burgled a bank
When nicked, was exceedingly frank
"You caught me tonight
Because I'm polite
And went back to ask who to thank".

> David Owen
> Shrewsbury, Shropshire

A burglar who burgled a bank
Drove a hole through the wall with a tank
To everyone's fury
He convinced a court jury
That his actions were merely a prank.

> Alan Badmington
> Abergavenny, Gwent

A CHEEKY TEA LADY FROM CREWE

A cheeky tea lady from Crewe
Was famed for her wonderful brew
But the secret, you see
In addition to tea
There was whisky and gin in it too.

> Betty Jones,
> Pembroke Dock, Dyfed

A cheeky tea lady from Crewe
Read cups for a selected few
When asked by Mike Flynn
If a fortune he'd win
Said "I see just limericks for you".

> Yvonne Courtney
> Llanelli, Dyfed

A cheeky tea lady from Crewe
Put rum in her eleven o'clock brew
Cooed her boss "You're a love
I feel light as a dove"
So saying—through the window he flew.

> Coral Courtney
> Llanelli, Dyfed

A cheeky tea lady from Crewe
Sold drinks which resembled shampoo
When a chap from the Gower
Used some in the shower
His thinning locks thickened and grew.

> J. Taylor
> Cwmbran

A YOUNG LAD FROM ABERGAVENNY

A young lad from Abergavenny
Yelled "Mummy, I've just spent a penny"
She pleaded with Pa
"Will you please stop this car
You've gone past one toilet too many".

> Harry Hartill
> Pontypridd, Mid Glam.

A young lad from Abergavenny
Was no use to a burglar called Benny
When he turned up to steal
With an old spinning wheel
Ben groaned "I said 'jemmy' not 'jenny' ".

> Ella Green
> Berkhamsted, Herts.

A young lad from Abergavenny
One evening, romantic as any
Rang Allison's bell
At Crossroads Motel
And everyone blamed it on Benny.

> Lucie Larstik
> Prestatyn, Clwyd.

A young lad from Abergavenny
By accident swallowed a penny
Indigestion ensued
And the wind it accrued
Which was only relieved by a Rennie.

> Daphne Davies,
> Abergavenny, Gwent

A BUGLER WHO BLEW IN THE BAND

A bugler who blew in the band
In his uniform looked very grand
Then one day when out marching
His wife put some starch in
Now his key is much higher than planned.

       W. J. Delve
       Swansea, West Glam.

A bugler who blew in the band
Found problems controlling his hand
To end this sad saga
He changed to a lager
Which reached parts, reached by no other brand.

       Winifred Pimlott
       Penmaenmawr, Gwynedd

A bugler who played in the band
Said "I'd better sit down, I'm half canned
But when the time comes
Though I'm tight as those drums
For God Shave the Queen, Shir, I'll shtand".

       Halina Day
       Cardiff, South Glam.

A bugler who played in the band
Thought he was the best in the land
But he learned his mistake
When, with mouth full of cake
What came out was not quite what he'd planned.

       Jean Oriel
       Mountain Ash, Mid Glam.

A PAINTER NAMED PETE FROM PENDINE

A painter named Pete from Pendine
Has married a cousin of mine
He's painted a rose
On each of her toes
And a 'Hands off, she's mine' on her spine.

> Teifion James
> Aberporth, Dyfed

A painter named Pete from Pendine
Was ordered to paint a white line
But that difficult fellow
Painted two, and both yellow
And was first to be caught with a fine.

> Marguerite Prisk
> Penarth, South Glam.

A painter called Pete from Pendine
Completed a house—it looked fine
But his happiness died
When the customer cried
"You've painted '16'—we're '9'.

> Dave Jackson
> Llantwit Major, South Glam.

A painter called Pete from Pendine
Gave the seats in the park a nice shine
But he ran out of luck
When two ladies got stuck
He'd not left a 'Wet Paint' warning sign.

> Ben Barker
> Llanelli, Dyfed

A BUXOM BARMAID FROM BRIDGEND

A buxom barmaid from Bridgend
With ease, iron bars she would bend
Her strength it was so
That she played second row
At the Brewery Field each weekend.

> Jason and Robert John
> Treorchy, Mid Glam.

A buxom barmaid from Bridgend
Would gentlemen clients befriend
With their eyes all agog
She would sell much more grog
And cause their right elbows to bend.

> A. C. Lewis
> Newport, Gwent

A buxom barmaid from Bridgend
Said "My job is not one I'd commend
I pull pints by the score
And then they want more
They're driving me right round the bend".

> Marguerite Prisk
> Penarth, South Glam.

A buxom barmaid from Bridgend
Has started a novel new trend
As she pours each man's drink
She will give him a wink
And a hint of a naughty weekend.

> Geraldine Richards
> Tywyn, Gwynedd

A COLWYN BAY GROCER SHUT SHOP

A Colwyn Bay grocer shut shop
When he dropped a large crate full of pop
Right on his big toe
So off he did go
To the Doc's hop, stop, hop, stop, hop, stop.

> Hilda Jones
> Penycae, Wrexham, Clwyd

A Colwyn Bay grocer shut shop
As profits reflected a drop
His prices for meat
Could never compete
With Tesco, Fine Fare or the Co-op.

> Marlene Kerr,
> Rhydlewis, Llandyssul, Dyfed

A Colwyn Bay grocer shut shop
And collapsed in a chair, fit to drop
He felt rather shaken
Surrounded by bacon
'Cos his slicer kept slicing non-stop

> Sue Sweeting
> Sarn, Newtown, Powys

A Colwyn Bay grocer shut shop
While he cleaned the place out with a mop
Where a stray dog called Bertie
Whose habits were dirty
Had caused more than takings to drop.

> Keith Coles
> Tondu, Bridgend, Mid Glamorgan

21

THERE WAS A YOUNG FELLOW FROM SPLOTT

There was a young fellow from Splott
Who planted spring bulbs in a pot
Though he'd waited all year
Not one bloom did appear
Said "Odd, they were all sixty watt".

> Marguerite Prisk
> Penarth, South Glam.

There was a young fellow from Splott
Who was really a bit of a clot
He put on a toga
To try out his yoga
And twisted himself in a knot.

> Jo Servini
> Penarth, South Glam.

There was a young fellow from Splott
Whose wife stuck her head in a pot
She turned it about
Then yelled through the spout
"Pass the milk love, this tea is too hot".

> Thelma Fox
> Porth, Mid Glam.

There was a young fellow from Splott
Who answered each question with "What?"
But his hearing was clear
When asked "Where's your beer?"
He would point to his empty pint pot.

> Harry Hartill
> Rhydyfelin, Pontypridd, Mid Glam.

A REFUSE COLLECTOR FROM ROSS

A refuse collector from Ross
Said "Rubbish is a gain not a loss
I've painted four chairs
The hall and the stairs
With a tin of discarded white gloss".

> Coral Courtney
> Llanelli, Dyfed

A refuse collector from Ross
Drove round like a young Stirling Moss
Scattered all of the bins
Hit the boss on the shins
He's a casualty now of job loss.

> Mary White
> Pontywaun, Crosskeys, Gwent

A refuse collector from Ross
With workmates would play 'pitch and toss'
The bins weren't collected
And as was expected
His cards he received from his boss.

> Dave Davies
> Griffithstown, Pontypool, Gwent

A refuse collector from Ross
Said loudly "I don't care a toss
If I fall head-first in
Any ashcart or bin
'Cos I'm covered for damage or loss".

> Kath Reed
> Middlezoy, Bridgwater, Somerset

AN ELDERLY FARMER FROM TENBY

An elderly farmer from Tenby
Drank gin from a cup made in Denbigh
But when the next day
He tried to cut hay
His legs were decidedly bendy.

> Jon Tovey
> Ilminster, Somerset

An elderly farmer from Tenby
Said "I'm old, but, I try to be trendy"
I play 'Nuts and May'
With the girls in the hay
But they have to be sixty to send me".

> Charles Latham
> Pwllheli, Gwynedd

An elderly farmer from Tenby
Said "What kind of a gun would a bren be?
Could I shoot all the rooks
Stealing corn from my stooks
A happier man, I would then be".

> Kenvyn Davies
> Brackla, Bridgend, Mid Glam.

An elderly farmer from Tenby
Cried "Inflation, oh what will the end be?
I pays more for me oil
Than I gets for me toil
And the pound's only worth about 10p".

> Mary Brunton
> Beeston, Nottingham

THERE WAS A GUITARIST CALLED BRETT

There was a guitarist called Brett
Who played for the swinging jet set
His guitar strings went ping
When he started to sing
Which caused the poor fellow to fret.

> Jean McIndo
> Abergavenny, Gwent

There was a guitarist called Brett
Who ate a guitar for a bet
His brother, more mellow
Consumed a large cello
But his tummy was rather upset.

> George Gidley
> Burnley, Lancs.

There was a guitarist called Brett
A collie he kept as a pet
When he played a new tune
It started to croon
They made a heart-warming duet.

> Olive Guidera
> Ruthin, Clwyd

There was a guitarist called Brett
One show he will want to forget
Whilst performing on stage
He went scarlet with rage
When his fingers got stuck in a fret.

> Audrey Lewis
> Mevagissey, Cornwall

28

A NOSEY OLD PARKER CALLED BARKER

A nosey old Parker called Barker
Annoyed his young neighbour, Miss Harker
When he peeped o'er the wall
On his bald head she'd scrawl
Rude signs in indelible marker.

> Sandra Sinclair
> Pembroke, Dyfed

A nosey old Parker called Barker
Took a holiday out in Lusaka
Though it wasn't done
He lay in the sun
Now he's older, much wiser and darker.

> J. Wright,
> Tynygongl, Gwynedd

A nosey old Parker called Barker
Though fond of his wife, used to nark her
By recording chit chat
On the walls of their flat
With a shocking pink, quick-dry ink marker.

> Alan Badmington
> Abergavenny, Gwent

A nosey old Parker called Barker
Saw a tank with a large 'Danger' marker
He just had to peep in
Now he's minus a chin
'Cos inside was an otter named Tarka.

> Mabs Watkins
> Taffs Well, South Glam.

A THRIFTY YOUNG TYPIST FROM TOWYN

A thrifty young typist from Towyn
Planned to marry her boy-friend called Owen
Her boss was quite smitten
By her notice—typewritten
"Please find someone else, 'cause I'm going".

> Dave Davies
> Griffithstown, Pontypool, Gwent

A thrifty young typist from Towyn
Split her skirt and was quick to start sewing
She stitched on a patch
In a cloth that would match
Thus preventing her 'secret' from showing.

> Geraldine Richards
> Tywyn, Gwynedd

A thrifty young typist from Towyn
Bought a cat from a chap named Magowan
Her wages, she blew
On tins of cat stew
To stop her dear puss from meowing.

> Jon Tovey
> Ilminster, Somerset

A thrifty young typist from Towyn
Shocked workmates by riding a cow in
She said "You may sneer
But petrol's so dear
And Dad doesn't need her for ploughing".

> Sandra Sinclair
> Pembroke, Dyfed

A LADY FROM LLANTWIT COULD SING

A lady from Llantwit could sing
Like an angel or lark on the wing
Then she had a sex change
Which affected her range
Now she sounds not like Bassey, but Bing.

> Eirwen Rogers
> Merthyr Tydfil, Mid Glam.

A lady from Llantwit could sing
While chewing a long piece of string
At a concert one night
She choked on a bite
In the middle of 'God Save the King'.

> Howard Gray
> Ynysybwl, Pontypridd, Mid Glam.

A lady from Llantwit could sing
Causing birds to migrate in the Spring
For she had such a voice
That they had little choice
But to fly all the way to Peking.

> Harry Meade
> Cymmer, Port Talbot, West Glam.

A lady from Llantwit could sing
So her voice through the valley should ring
But the sound she thought charming
Was rather alarming
And the cats to her doorstep would bring.

> Pauline Knight
> Abergavenny, Gwent

THERE ONCE WAS A YOUNG GIRL CALLED PENNY

There once was a young girl called Penny
Who married a boy from Ewenny
The life that they led
Was mostly in bed
And their children were ever so many.

> Harry Hartill
> Rhydyfelin, Pontypridd, Mid Glam.

There once was a young girl called Penny
Who flirted with all in Llangenny
She started with Bill
Then Arthur and Phil
And finished with Mike, John and Lennie.

> Alan Badmington
> Abergavenny, Gwent

There once was a young girl called Penny
Who travelled to Abergavenny
When she got on the bus
She created a fuss
'Cos there wasn't a seat, no not any.

> G. F. Bell
> Rhydyfelin, Pontypridd, Mid Glam.

There once was a young girl called Penny
Her morals?—she didn't have any
But she was, all agree
(And that includes me)
A source of great comfort to many.

> Brian E. Wood
> Creigiau, Nr. Cardiff, South Glam.

A POPULAR POP STAR FROM PANDY

A popular pop star from Pandy
Was considered a bit of a dandy
When he sang in the mike
He sat on a bike
So the fans wouldn't know he was bandy.

> M. Mathews
> Merthyr Tydfil, Mid Glam.

A popular pop star from Pandy
Whose first name was Tony—that's handy
Said he at a gig
"You'll know why I'm big
It's so easy to say Tonypandy".

> H. Lee
> Rumney, Cardiff, South Glam.

A popular pop star from Pandy
In tight jeans looks ever so bandy
While twisting in song
He did something wrong
And since has been known as Sandy.

> Alan Jones
> Pontywaun, Gwent

A popular pop star from Pandy
Changed her name from Angharad to Mandy
Astronomical fame
Didn't come with the same
But for her, a poor speller, 'twas handy.

> M. Mathews
> Merthyr Tydfil, Mid Glam.

A COAL MERCHANT FROM COLWYN BAY

A coal merchant from Colwyn Bay
Fell in love with a lady called May
Whom he tried to excite
With some free anthracite
But she bought a gas fire, next day.

> W. J. Delve
> West Cross, Swansea, West Glam

A coal merchant from Colwyn Bay
Grew rich, in one year and a day
He bought a Rolls Royce
Then in a posh voice
Said "Who says that grime doesn't pay?"

> Coral Courtney
> Llanelli, Dyfed

A coal merchant from Colwyn Bay
Decided to work Christmas Day
But because it was Yule
He couldn't get fuel
So Santa delivered by sleigh.

> Geoff Marston
> Monmouth, Gwent

A coal merchant from Colwyn Bay
On the 'phone once was o'erheard to say
"That's all very fine
It's no fault of mine
I sell it, not dig it—good day".

> M. C. Edwards
> Gilfachrheda, New Quay, Dyfed

A COTTAGER LIVING AT CLATTER

A cottager living at Clatter
Went out for a pint and a natter
His wife said "Now Jack
Don't be late getting back
Or your lunch will be cold on the platter".

> Liz Taylor
> Coventry, West Midlands

A cottager living at Clatter
Thought fruit was the juice that should matter
He drank it for dinner
And grew a lot thinner
While everyone else got much fatter.

> L. Burchell
> Tredegar, Gwent

A cottager living at Clatter
Had a voice that got flatter and flatter
He went into Clwyd
And drank some Jeyes Fluid
And that was the end of the matter.

> Rodney Richard Ash
> Okehampton, Devon

A cottager living at Clatter
Jazzed up a Beethoven sonata
His great uncle Hubert
Calypsoed to Schubert
And tap danced to Bach's last cantata.

> Deric John
> Cwmbach, Aberdare, Mid Glam.

A HANDSOME YOUNG BOATMAN FROM SKYE

A handsome young boatman from Skye
Had an anchor tattooed on his thigh
When asked by a miss
The reason for this
He replied "I'll not be left high and dry".

> Kenneth Courtney
> Llanelli, Dyfed

A handsome young boatman from Skye
Plied his oars with a sob and a sigh
"I don't mind the water"
He told the Laird's daughter
"But I do like to keep my kilt dry".

> Molly Taylor
> Wrexham, Clwyd

A handsome young boatman from Skye
Sailed off with a glint in his eye
He left from the quay
With a girl on his knee
And in full Scottish voice, yelled "Och Aye".

> Ros Grant
> Abergavenny, Gwent

A handsome young boatman from Skye
Decided to learn how to fly
"If I'd come by boat
I'd still be afloat"
He cried, as he fell from the sky.

> Anon
> Moelfre

A BUSY YOUNG BAKER FROM BARRY

A busy young baker from Barry
Said "My loaves are as hard as old Harry
If I try yeast instead
Of this compound of lead
They'll be lighter and easy to carry".

> Guy Dawson
> Swansea, West Glam.

A busy young baker from Barry
Was shouting in panic for Gary
The oven had slammed
His pinny was jammed
And he'd ruined his chances to marry.

> Jean Wrigley
> Widnes, Cheshire

A busy young baker from Barry
When asked if one day he would marry
Said "The answer is no
'Cos I'm kneading more dough
To start up my own cash and carry".

> Charles Latham
> Pwllheli, Gwynedd

A busy young Baker from Barry
Told her boyfriend that they should soon marry
When he asked "What's the rush?"
She replied with a blush
"There's a bun in the oven, dear Larry".

> G. Gidley
> Burnley, Lancs.

A FUSSY OLD GARDENER FROM SLADE

A fussy old gardener from Slade
Cut a worm right in half with his spade
When he saw the disaster
He repaired it with plaster
And the worm wriggled off in band-aid.

> Enid Foscolo
> Barry, South Glam.

A fussy old gardener from Slade
Grew lemons to make lemonade
It didn't taste nice
So he added some spice
It's amazing the difference it made.

> Jon Tovey
> Ilminster, Somerset

A fussy old gardener from Slade
Was worried his flowers would fade
So he utilised dye
Now his neighbours ask why
The blossoms look really handmade.

> Jane Welsh
> Catchems End, Bewdley, Worcs.

A fussy old gardener from Slade
Grew veg of a very high grade
If a slug dared to show
He attacked with his hoe
And added a notch on his spade.

> Olwen Dilloway
> Prestatyn, Clwyd

A BUTTERFLY COLLECTOR CALLED HECTOR

A butterfly collector called Hector
Strayed into a dense woodland sector
He found, with regret
That he'd caught in his net
A fire-fly with rear-end reflector.

> M. M. Boomsma-Williams
> Pen-y-bont-fawr, Nr. Oswestry, Salop

A butterfly collector called Hector
Had a penchant for sweet things like nectar
He knelt on his knees
To study some bees
And was stung in his own private sector.

> Marshall Hopla
> St. Brides Major, Bridgend, Mid Glam.

A butterfly collector called Hector
Owns a banger he's christened 'Perfecta'
One fine summer day
While stalking his prey
He crashed poor Perfecta and wrecked her.

> Linda Garrett
> Caerleon, Newport, Gwent

A butterfly collector called Hector
Once went to the West German sector
Where he and a pal
Caught a Red Admiral
A rare Iron Curtain defector.

> Alan Badmington
> Abergavenny, Gwent

A LITTLE OLD LADY CALLED NELLIE

A little old lady called Nellie
Had a cobra tattooed on her belly
Its head caused alarm
As it curled round her arm
And its tail disappeared down her welly.

> Dave Jackson
> Llantwit Major, South Glam.

A little old lady called Nellie
Met a little old man from Pwllheli
At ninety and eighty
They got very matey
But all they could do was watch telly.

> Jean McIndo
> Abergavenny, Gwent

A little old lady called Nellie
Was arrested for stealing a jelly
Amid struggles and yells
She was placed in the cells
Demanding to see Petrocelli.

> Alan Badmington
> Abergavenny, Gwent

A little old lady called Nellie
Is frequently seen on the telly
She is known to report
On all kinds of sport
From football to throwing the welly.

> Jason and Robert John
> Treorchy, Mid Glam.

A DIRTY OLD SHEEPDOG CALLED BOOT

A dirty old sheepdog called Boot
More often than not, looked a brute
But a session of grooming
Would leave his coat blooming
And the poodle next door thought him cute.

Geraldine Richards
Ffordd Dyfed, Tywyn, Gwynedd

A dirty old sheepdog called Boot
Had an owner as daft as a coot
They worked in the dark
And instead of a bark
The old boy taught Boot how to hoot.

W. H. Prosser
Yeovil, Somerstt

A dirty old sheepdog called Boot
Each lamp post he passed would pollute
One day he got free
And watered a tree
Which rotted away at the root.

Jane Shearer Parry
Nannerch, Mold, Clwyd

A dirty old sheepdog called Boot
One evening got drunk as a newt
It wasn't the whisky
Which made him feel frisky
But an extra large bottle of Brut.

Alan Badmington
Abergavenny, Gwent

A SAILOR WHO SAILED OVERSEAS

A sailor who sailed overseas
Ignored all his mates' urgent pleas
He then climbed up the mast
And for one month did fast
Only swallowing insects and bees.

      Coral Courtney
      Llanelli, Dyfed

A sailor who sailed overseas
Always prayed for a bit of a breeze
When asked why, he just grinned
And replied " 'Cos the wind
Lifts the dress and exposes the knees".

      Brian E. Wood
      Creigiau, Nr. Cardiff, South Glam.

A sailor who sailed overseas
Had a wife and ten kids in Crosskeys
Twelve more in Japan
And a few in Taiwan
No wonder he walked on his knees.

      Hilda Jones
      Penycae, Wrexham, Clwyd

A sailor who sailed overseas
Had girls names tattoed on his knees
While taking out Sue
He had to hide 'Pru'
But sometimes wore shorts, just to tease.

      Maralyn Olsen
      Brithdir, New Tredegar, Mid Glam.

A COWBOY WHO HAILED FROM THE PRAIRIE

A cowboy who hailed from the prairie
Had a moustache—luxuriant and hairy
He let the thing grow
'Til one end touched his toe
And the other reached Abertillery.

> Eryl Griffiths
> Wrexham, Clwyd

A cowboy who hailed from the prairie
Had a girl friend, Calamity Mary
She said "What a twirp
You're no Wyatt Earp
In fact, you're a bit of a fairy".

> E. W. Delve
> West Cross, Swansea, West Glam.

A cowboy who hailed from the prairie
He was big, he was mean, he was hairy
But sad to relate
He fell foul of Kate
Who filled him with lead in the dairy.

> C. Hamilton
> Llandaff, Cardiff, South Glam.

A cowboy who hailed from the prairie
Thought gun-play a bit hairy-fairy
'Til a rustler's six-shooter
Took a lump off his hooter
Now of guns, he's exceedingly wary.

> Paul Walsh
> Llandough, Penarth, South Glam.

A REGAL YOUNG LADY NAMED DI

A regal young lady named Di
Said "I can't bake, cook, boil or fry"
Charles replied "Well I feel
If we both need a meal
We'll just give the Palace a try".

> Bob Wolfson
> Cardiff, South Glam.

A regal young lady named Di
Plans to wed at the end of July
Now the daily routine
Of the young future queen
Is to practise "MY HUSBAND AND I".

> Alan Badmington
> Abergavenny, Gwent

A regal young lady named Di
Retorted quite angrily "Why"
When asked by the press
Where she'd bought her dress
"Would I ask you where you bought your tie?"

> Jean Jones
> Llangammarch Wells, Powys

A regal young lady named Di
As the time of her wedding drew nigh
Said to Charles, on the course
"If you fall off your horse
Try to keep in one piece for July".

> Anne Treharne
> Tonyrefail, Mid Glam.

A CRAFTY OLD CROOK FROM CAERPHILLY

A crafty old crook from Caerphilly
Who was known to the locals as Billy
Once pick-locked a door
Then shouted "Good lor
I've burgled my own house, how silly".

J. Ash
Ely, Cardiff, South Glam.

A crafty old crook from Caerphilly
Used to steal odds and ends, willy-nilly
But one day in a shop
He was caught by a cop
And now he's on dry bread and skilly.

George Lewis
Claines, Worcester

A crafty old crook from Caerphilly
Stole a kiss from a nifty young filly
With a fistful of zest
She laid him to rest
In the moat, where he floats like a lily.

John Roberts
Llangwm, Usk, Gwent

A crafty old crook from Caerphilly
Had a yearning to do something silly
He drove into a bank
In a Scorpion tank
But is now in a cell, cold and chilly.

Ken Jones
Milford Haven, Dyfed

A SUPER SLIM STARLET FROM SOLVA

A super slim starlet from Solva
Had a Latin producer called Yolva
When he went down to see her
He said "Mama mia
If you eata much less, you'll dissolva".

E. M. Lewis
Port Talbot, West Glam.

A super slim starlet from Solva
Bought a very big shiny revolver
And just for a bet
She played Russian Roulette
In their choir, now the angels involve her.

Mary Mathews
Merthyr Tydfil, Mid Glam.

A super slim starlet from Solva
Stopped eating to save for a Volva
She became oh so thin
That on taking aspirin
The pain killing tablet dissolved her.

Coral Courtney
Llanelli, Dyfed

A super slim starlet from Solva
On knees asked the priest to absolve her
He quickly said "Yes"
Then he heard her confess
She'd shot J.R. with her revolver.

John Lodwick
Tutshill, Chepstow, Gwent

A CHEMIST FROM CARDIGAN BAY

A chemist from Cardigan Bay
Invented a Welsh leek hairspray
But it did not sell well
On account of the smell
And the fact that it turned your hair grey.

> Hilda Jones
> Penycae, Wrexham

A chemist from Cardigan Bay
Put a new slimming aid on display
This talking device
Offered subtle advice
Such as "Get off, you're too fat to weigh".

> Alan Badmington
> Abergavenny, Gwent

A chemist from Cardigan Bay
Committed a faux pas one day
He gave the wrong pill
To a girl who was ill
Now they're calling her Fred and not May.

> R. Evans
> Llanelli, Dyfed

A chemist from Cardigan Bay
Was heard to remark in dismay
"I haven't a clue
If this script is Urdu
Sanscrit or a map of Bombay".

> Tom Adams Jones
> Wrexham

AN ELDERLY RECTOR FROM RHYL

An elderly rector from Rhyl
Received an enormous gas bill
He said with a fright
"Now this can't be right
We've oil, so the bill should be nil".

C. E. Harper
Stamford, Lincs.

An elderly rector from Rhyl
Said "I'm tired of hearing 'I will'
I wish they'd arrange
To say 'Won't' for a change
It really would give me a thrill".

E. B. Jones
Dowlais, Mid Glam.

An elderly rector from Rhyl
Whose church was decidedly chill
Decided at Mass
To turn up the gas
'Twas not lit—now they're reading his will.

Betty Fowles
Port Talbot, West Glam.

An elderly rector from Rhyl
Admired the poet called Will
He set off for Stratford
But ended in Catford
For his sense of direction was nil.

Marion Bodger
Bangor-on-Dee, Clwyd

53

A HOT AIR BALLOONIST FROM BARRY

A hot air balloonist from Barry
Left Cardiff for Weston, to marry
The wind blew the wrong way
So instead he wed May
Whom he met, when he crashed in Llanharry.

> Irene Dando
> Pencoed, Bridgend, Mid Glam.

A hot air balloonist from Barry
Had a little Welsh dragon named Larry
Who gave plenty of heat
On a diet of peat
'Til he ran out of fuel in Glengarry.

> J. Williams
> Haverfordwest, Dyfed

A hot air balloonist from Barry
When up in the air, he would carry
A spare can of gas
But one day alas
He forgot he had lent it to Harry.

> Ted Callaghan
> Reynoldstone, Swansea, West Glam.

A hot air balloonist from Barry
Too long in the sky tried to tarry
He ran out of gas
Landed 'splat' on the grass
What a way to commit Hari Kari.

> June Smithers
> Llanwrda, Dyfed

A FLORIST WHO FLAUNTED HER FLOWERS

A florist who flaunted her flowers
Often polished the petals for hours
She never used Vim
To keep them in trim
After learning it bleaches and scours.

> Alan Badmington
> Abergavenny, Gwent

A florist who flaunted her flowers
Was caught in two very sharp showers
To ruin her day
Her blooms blew away
And her nose ran for twenty four hours.

> W. J. Delve
> West Cross, Swansea, West Glam.

A florist who flaunted her flowers
On a window display, she spent hours
Then a madman dashed in
What a crash!—What a din!
'Twas that Basil (not Brush) . . Fawlty Towers.

> Winifred Prinlott
> Penmaenmawr, Gwynedd

A florist who flaunted her flowers
Would brag of their fragrantic powers
Till a poodle called Meg
Came and lifted its leg
Now each bloom doesn't freshen but sours.

> G. Edwards
> Gurnos, Merthyr Tydfil, Mid Glam.

THERE WAS A STRANGE FELLOW FROM ROME

There was a strange fellow from Rome
Who smelled a gas leak at his home
To find it, the blighter
Ignited his lighter
And landed on St. Peter's Dome.

> Alan Badmington
> Abergavenny, Gwent

There was a strange fellow from Rome
A barber with scissors and comb
In a shaky falsetto
He sang Rigoletto
As he lathered his clients with foam.

> J. Wright
> Tynygongl, Gwynedd

There was a strange fellow from Rome
All covered in lather and foam
Who thought it was posh
Driving through a car wash
To polish his chariot's chrome.

> Len Griffiths
> Woolavington, Bridgwater, Somerset

There was a strange fellow from Rome
Whose head was a round shiny dome
But he saw the bright side
And to jeers replied
"Well at least I've no need of a comb".

> Jean Oriel
> Mountain Ash, Mid Glam.

A BOLD BRIGADIER FROM BRECON

A bold brigadier from Brecon
Thought the Beacons were just there to trek on
He got lost on a peak
And was gone for a week
They should buy him a compass, I reckon.

W. E. Moore
Caerphilly, Mid Glam.

A bold brigadier from Brecon
Went looking for things he could check on
And one thing he found
That was lying around
Was the block Anne Boleyn put her neck on.

Betty Jones
Pembroke Dock, Dyfed

A bold brigadier from Brecon
Would follow where ere love would beckon
He'd be tempted to kiss
Each sweet shy young miss
When the camp put their own discotheque on.

Betty Jones
Pembroke Dock, Dyfed

A bold brigadier from Brecon
On his wife's moods he could never reckon
So one sunny day
He went on his way
To his girl-friend in old Llanfairfechan.

Dora Peters
Deganwy, Gwynedd

A LOVELY PLUMP TURKEY IN WALES

A lovely plump turkey in Wales
Was born with two heads and two tails
With two parsons' noses
And heads, one supposes
It will be quite a wow at the sales.

> Mary C. Edwards
> Gilfachrheda, New Quay, Dyfed

A lovely plump turkey in Wales
Didn't care for the snow and the gales
Or the gay festive season
And so, for this reason
Flew south with some friendly females.

> Margaret Blythe
> Prestatyn, Clwyd

A lovely plump turkey in Wales
Ran away o'er the hills and the dales
The cause of his puffing
Was a fear of stuffing
And a longing to live and tell tales.

> Olive Paddington
> Pembroke Dock, Dyfed

A lovely plump turkey in Wales
Was favourite to win at the sales
With a forty inch chest
It outclassed the rest
The others just tickled the scales.

> Leslie Henson
> Llandudno, Gwynedd

TWO PRETTY YOUNG LADIES FROM BUDE

Two pretty young ladies from Bude
When spending a penny, they queued
But the notice was faint
That spelled out 'Wet Paint'
And found to the seats they were glued.

> Coral Courtney
> Llanelli, Dyfed

Two pretty young ladies from Bude
Once went for a swim in the nude
Along came a shark
Who made a tooth mark
But where, I can't say, it's too rude.

> Alan Witcombe
> Brecon, Powys

Two pretty young ladies from Bude
Retained all the gum that they chewed
When re-cycled in tanks
It was sold to the Yanks
A process both cunning and shrewd.

> J. W. Evans
> Abertridwr, Mid Glam.

Two pretty young ladies from Bude
When swimming neglected their food
In the 31st week
When they played hide and seek
They were looked for but couldn't be viewed.

> Alan James
> Newport, Gwent

A RADIO HAM FROM PEKING

A radio ham from Peking
Used to tune to pop music and swing
But one day a loose wire
Caused his set to catch fire
And now he can't hear a damn thing.

> George Lewis
> Claines, Worcs.

A radio ham from Peking
Was really incredibly thin
His friend said "Take care
Don't sit over there
Or, in error, you may get plugged in".

> Eileen Brown
> Six Bells, Abertillery, Gwent

A radio ham from Peking
Who thought that he really could sing
Once fractured his pelvis
While doing an Elvis
The hip-swaying, rock and roll 'King'.

> George Bonter
> Cardiff, South Glam.

A radio ham from Peking
Once turned out for Wales on the wing
When starved of a pass
He sat on the grass
And tuned in to listen to Bing.

> Roberta David
> Cardigan, Dyfed

A CADDIE WHO CAME FROM CATHAYS

A caddie who came from Cathays
Gained a very raw golfer's high praise
By carrying supplies
Of beer and meat pies
To a bloke who'd been bunkered for days.

> Dennis Collins
> Wirral, Merseyside

A caddie who came from Cathays
Drove to work in a deep drunken haze
When the cops stopped his car
He was six over par
"Now you'll just drive a ball", the judge says.

> John Halstead
> Caernarfon, Gwynedd

A caddie who came from Cathays
Held a match up with trivial delays
Then his golfer saw red
Wrapped a club round his head
He's in hospital now for X rays.

> Betty Fowler
> Port Talbot, West Glam.

A caddie who came from Cathays
Remarked "It's been one of those days
With landscapers in force
Redesigning the course
And now it's like Hampton Court Maze".

> Ella Green
> Berkhamsted, Herts.

A RUGBY ELEVEN FROM CEFN

A rugby eleven from Cefn
Turned up for a match down in Devon
Seems two couldn't play
And one went astray
While another was working 'til seven.

> B. A. Edwards
> Bontnewydd, Caernarfon

A rugby eleven from Cefn
Once fielded a full back named Bevan
He kicked a conversion
But used such exertion
That the ball landed somewhere in Devon.

> Pat King
> Caerphilly, Mid Glam.

A rugby eleven from Cefn
Not a genuine fifteen or seven
Their ball, I'll be bound
Is not oval but round
And their hero, not Gareth, but Kevin.

> B. B. Davies
> Haverfordwest, Dyfed

A rugby eleven from Cefn
All died and went straight up to hefn
But St. Peter said "Back
You're not a full pack
Get 'lefn more men—minus sefn".

> Robert S. John
> Aberdare, Mid Glam.

A YOUNG WREXHAM SCHOOLBOY OF TEN

A young Wrexham schoolboy of ten
Fell in love with his teacher, Miss Venn
He said "Be my spouse
You can live in our house
And help with my sums now and then".

> G. Davies
> Three Crosses, Swansea, West Glam.

A young Wrexham schoolboy of ten
For a cute little girl had a yen
And gave her sweet looks
And carried her books
'Til she dated his best friend named Len.

> Joy Evans
> Newport, Gwent

A young Wrexham schoolboy of ten
Was 'mitching' from school once again
"Dear teacher", he wrote
"Mother's writing this note
'Cos I'm ill and I can't hold a pen".

> Keith Coles
> Tondu, Bridgend, Mid Glam.

A young Wrexham schoolboy of ten
Was chasing his grandpa's prize hen
Was told "You gone seven
But you won't reach eleven
If you ever do that again".

> Mabs Watkins
> Taff's Well, Cardiff, South Glam.

A SHIFTY SCRAP DEALER FROM SALE

A shifty scrap dealer from Sale
When in court tried to pitch such a tale
He claimed that the lead
From the magistrates' shed
Fell onto his cart in the gale.

>   Glyn Edwards
>   Merthyr Tydfil, Mid Glam.

A shifty scrap dealer from Sale
Acquired some ten miles of rail
Between Neath and Bridgend
'left a gap on a bend
So the law came and put him in gaol.

>   Ella Green
>   Berkhamsted, Herts.

A shifty scrap dealer from Sale
Had eyesight which started to fail
When the police came to look
At his sales receipt book
They found all the entries in braille.

>   Alan Badmington
>   Abergavenny, Gwent

A shifty scrap dealer from Sale
In his lunch hour delivered the mail
At the end of his round
The poor chap found
That his sandwiches had all gone stale.

>   Howard Gray
>   Ynysybwl, Pontypridd, Mid Glam.

A DRAGON WHO HAD TOO MUCH DRINK

A dragon who had too much drink
A good sport, no doubt, don't you think?
But the court thought him silly
When he sprayed Piccadilly
And made all the passers-by blink.

> G. Davies
> Three Crosses, Swansea, West Glam.

A dragon who had too much drink
Had to spend Friday night in the clink
Still he got to the game
Which Wales lost, what a shame
'Could have done with his fire, don't you think?

> Patricia Rees
> Cwmparc, Treorchy, Mid Glamorgan

A dragon who had too much drink
In London caused rather a stink
His public Welsh leak
Brought rebuke from a beak
£10, and a night in the clink.

> Alan Badmington
> Abergavenny, Gwent

A dragon who had too much drink
Heard a Cockney say "Guvnor oi fink
Oi'll go on the wagon
Oi've seen a red dragon
And the elephants here are all pink".

> Jeff Williams
> Bargoed, Mid Glamorgan

A BACHELOR FARMER FROM MOLD

A bachelor farmer from Mold
Sang bass in a voice of pure gold
But he sat down one day
On a pitch-fork, they say
Now he's singing soprano, I'm told.

> B. Wright,
> address unknown

A bachelor farmer from Mold
Kept his cattle inside from the cold
He knitted his flocks
Some lovely red socks
While his pigs hog the fire 'til they're sold.

> Charles Latham,
> Pwllheli

A bachelor farmer from Mold
Found the night-time was getting too cold
So he warmed up his life
By taking a wife
And increased his stock many fold.

> Eryl Griffiths,
> Wrexham, Clwyd

A bachelor farmer from Mold
Had hands that were terribly cold
He said to his herd
"Though it may sound absurd
Just jump up and down while I hold".

> M. Phillips
> Llandaff North, Cardiff, South Glam.

A FRIGID BRIDGE FAN FROM CWMBRAN

A frigid bridge fan from Cwmbran
Couldn't bear to be touched by a man
So while she was playing
She just kept on saying
"Please pass me the cards in a pan".

> Anna Owens
> Kidderminster, Worcs.

A frigid bridge fan from Cwmbran
Said "Omar Sharif is all man
He's skilful and nice
And could thaw inch-thick ice
So I watch him when ever I can".

> Charles Latham
> Pwllheli, Gwynedd

A frigid bridge fan from Cwmbran
To play, wore a flowing Kaftan
She said with a smile
"It's well worth my while
For I hide cards and cheat when I can".

> Coral Courtney
> Llanelli, Dyfed

A frigid bridge fan from Cwmbran
Played bridge on her fridge from a plan
The fridge froze her bridge
And her partner called Midge
Made use of a de-icer can.

> Jane Welsh
> Bewdley, Worcs.

WHILE OUT ON HIS BIKE FOR A RIDE

While out on his bike for a ride
To reach a high speed, grandad tried
He went such a pace
That he joined the Milk Race
Now he wears the lead jersey with pride.

> Audrey Kenny
> Grangetown, Cardiff, South Glam.

While out on his bike for a ride
An ugly old hag Fred espied
She said "I've a tandem
Which I'll ride at random
With one who will make me his bride".

> Bill Jenkins
> Newport, Gwent

While out on his bike for a ride
A burglar, his jemmy did hide
But he came a cropper
When he knocked down a copper
Now he's spending his Christmas inside.

> Edith Knight
> Lewistown, Ogmore Vale, South Glam.

While out on his bike for a ride
He started to slither and slide
Through the front door he fell
Of a local hotel
And ordered a fish and french fried.

> J. Wright
> Tynygongl, Gwynedd

A CHEEKY CHAR LADY FROM CHIRK

A cheeky char lady from Chirk
Took a great deal of pride in her work
She polished the town
Then without grouse or frown
Scrubbed the motorway up to Falkirk.

Lewis Price
Cheltenham, Glos.

A cheeky char lady from Chirk
Told a friend as they travelled to work
"You may think that your turban
Makes you look quite suburban
But I think you resemble a Turk".

D. Hampton
Rhydyfelin, Pontypridd, Mid Glam.

A cheeky char lady from Chirk
Ceased her toil for the day with a jerk
For she met a sad end
As she slipped round the bend
Of the toilet she cleaned whilst at work.

George Lewis
Claines, Worcester

A cheeky char lady from Chirk
Was asked why she went out to work
She said "With my spouse
Just to get from the house
To me, it's not work, but a perk".

Audrie Jones
Bulwark, Chepstow, Gwent

A PORTER FROM PORT TALBOT STATION

A porter from Port Talbot station
Loved steam trains with such dedication
That he stood on the funnel
As it went through a tunnel
Now friends call him Dai Capitation.

> Cynthia Large
> Beddau, Pontypridd, Mid Glam.

A porter from Port Talbot station
Caused the public a deal of vexation
When he carried their bags
He'd demand twenty fags
As well as a hefty donation.

> Halina Day
> Cardiff, South Glam.

A porter from Port Talbot station
Doesn't think much of train sanitation
Folk will not refrain
From pulling the chain
While stationary at that location.

> Alan Badmington
> Abergavenny, Gwent

A porter from Port Talbot station
Gave passengers wrong information
He'd send some to Bridgend
And some to Land's End
But never the right destination.

> Coral Courtney
> Llanelli, Dyfed

A PEMBROKESHIRE FARMER FROM DALE

A Pembrokeshire farmer from Dale
Couldn't see how his business could fail
He fed the cows pins
So the milk came in tins
Which cut out the churns and the pail.

> S Reardon
> Liverpool, Merseyside

A Pembrokeshire farmer from Dale
Went swimming in search of a whale
The sea was so rough
That he ran out of puff
And could neither inhale or exhale.

> Eirlys Mitchell
> Sheffield

A Pembrokeshire farmer from Dale
Had trouble in growing good kale
He sent for Welsh muck
Which brought him more luck
Now he's selling the stuff by the bale.

> Patricia Underhill
> Quinton, Birmingham, West Midlands

A Pembrokeshire farmer from Dale
Found his crops were beginning to fail
So he sold all his horses
And joined the Armed Forces
Which was better than going to jail.

> Charles Latham
> Pwllheli, Gwynedd

A SURGEON WHO SUNNED ON THE SAND

A surgeon who sunned on the sand
Had a smile exceedingly bland
Then a blonde came along
Wearing only a thong
And the rest, I'm afraid, has been banned.

> Richard Spring
> Cotham, Bristol, Avon

A surgeon who sunned on the sand
Fell asleep to the strains of a band
He dreamt vivid visions
Of former incisions
When he woke, he was minus a hand.

> Alan Badmington
> Abergavenny, Gwent

A surgeon who sunned on the sand
Was covered with oil and well tanned
His costume was brief
No more than a leaf
To cover what's called 'No man's land'.

> Teifion James
> Parcllyn, Cardigan, Dyfed

A surgeon who sunned on the sand
Relaxed to the local brass band
When he saw above
A rather large dove
Then felt something land on his hand.

> Jean Mann
> Llanover, Abergavenny, Gwent

A FIREMAN NOW STATIONED AT FLINT

A fireman now stationed at Flint
From his workmates would not take a hint
He directed the hose
At the Fire Chief's nose
Now he's bruised and his arm's in a splint.

> Glyn Edwards
> Gurnos, Merthyr Tydfil, Mid Glam.

A fireman now stationed at Flint
At Newmarket found himself skint
Put his shirt on a horse
And lost it of course
His language was too bad to print.

> Harry Hartill
> Rhydyfelin, Pontypridd, Mid Glam.

A fireman now stationed at Flint
Is possessed of a terrible squint
He said "I'm O.K.
If I'm told where to spray
I can get through the hole in a mint".

> M. Cole
> Colwyn Bay, Clwyd

A fireman now stationed at Flint
In his eyes had a lecherous glint
As higher and higher
He climbed to the fire
To rescue a sexy young bint.

> Murray Jenkins
> Coity, Bridgend, Mid Glam.

THERE WAS AN OLD LADY FROM GWENT

There was an old lady from Gwent
Whose nose was so long and so bent
It began near her lip
Turned round by her hip
Then, nobody knows where it went

> Jan Plested
> Rhyd Ddu, Nr. Caernarfon, Gwynedd

There was an old lady from Gwent
Who went to a toilet in Kent
She stood at the door
For ten minutes or more
Then discovered her penny was bent.

> Lawrence Selby
> Tonyrefail, Porth, Mid Glam.

There was an old lady from Gwent
Who covered herself with cheap scent
When friends asked her why
She made this reply
"It helps me to know where I went".

> J. Carr
> Menai Bridge

There was an old lady from Gwent
Who was grateful her life was mis-spent
With good common sense
She'd kept evidence
Now blackmailing pays off her rent.

> M. M. Roach
> Haverfordwest, Dyfed

A DARING AND DASHING YOUNG DANE

A daring and dashing young Dane
Had women and booze on the brain
His idea of bliss
Was a pint and a kiss
Now at nineteen, he's feeling the strain.

W. J. Delve
West Cross, Swansea, West Glam.

A daring and dashing young Dane
Chased a pretty young girl down a lane
Did he catch her?—no fear
Know what happened, my dear
He tripped up and fell down a drain.

J. B. Laughton
Ruthin, Clwyd

A daring and dashing young Dane
Woke up in considerable pain
A night out on lager
Began this sad saga
He swears he won't do it again.

Ella Green
Berkhamsted, Herts.

A daring and dashing young Dane
In the week dates Priscilla and Jane
But every weekend
He chooses to spend
With Helena, Pam or Elaine.

Alan Badmington
Abergavenny, Gwent

A DASHING YOUNG MILKMAN NAMED DAI

A dashing young milikman named Dai
Was known as a real ladies' guy
He gave every miss
A pint for a kiss
And more for a whole week's supply.

> Bill Burrows,
> Newport, Gwent

A dashing young milkman named Dai
When playing for Wales, scored a try
The cheers of his team
Woke him from the dream
And he went on his rounds with a sigh.

> Adrienne Palmer
> Maesycoed, Pontypridd, Mid Glam.

A dashing young milkman named Dai
Thought a do-it-yourself stunt he'd try
So he swopped his milk float
For a young nanny goat
But his nanny was Billy—and dry.

> M. M. Roach
> Haverfordwest, Dyfed

A dashing young milkman named Dai
Loved to give all the ladies the eye
When they answered his ring
Wearing hardly a thing
He would slip them some cream on the sly.

> Jean Oriel
> Mountain Ash, Mid Glam.

WHEN GRANDMA DRANK TOO MUCH SHERRY

When grandma drank too much sherry
Her face turned as red as a cherry
She stood on her head
Then fell out of bed
And landed headfirst in the jerry.

> Michael Roberts
> Corwen, Clwyd

When grandma drank too much sherry
At a Christmas Eve party in Derry
She caught the wrong bus
And started to cuss
When she found it was destined for Kerry.

> P. Knowles
> Manchester

When grandma drank too much sherry
It went to her head, made her merry
She grabbed her poor spouse
Rock and rolled round the house
While her little nose glowed like a cherry.

> Betty Fowles
> Port Talbot, West Glam.

When grandma drank too much sherry
A doctor became necessary
"If you don't stick to tea
Your name we shall see
In the newspaper's obituary".

> Joan Salisbury
> Southport, Merseyside

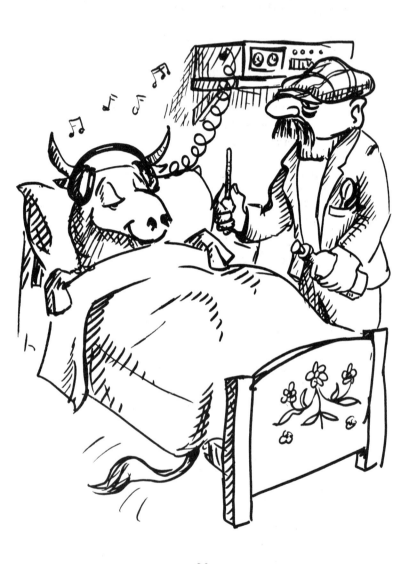

A FARMER FROM GILWERN CALLED DAI

A farmer from Gilwern called Dai
Grew rich raising barley and rye
When he died, locals said
"Though he never got wed
He sowed his wild oats on the sly".

> Marguerite Prisk
> Penarth, South Glam.

A farmer from Gilwern called Dai
Had a pig which he taught how to fly
With his wife and son Mark
They flew over Arms Park
And watched the big match from the sky.

> Harry Hartill
> Rhydyfelin, Pontyridd, Mid Glam.

A farmer from Gilwern called Dai
Was really a very nice guy
When his cows became sick
He would play them music
Now he goes by the name 'Dai Hi-Fi'.

> E. Lewis
> Port Talbot, West Glam.

A farmer from Gilwern called Dai
Saw a cow flying high in the sky
He said "What a sight
A cow in mid-flight!
I'll have to stop drinking that rye.

> Phillip Ware
> Blaengwynfi, Port Talbot, West Glam.

A RADIO WALES LISTENER FROM HOLT

A Radio Wales listener from Holt
Who dreamed she was riding a colt
Let out a loud cry
"This fence is too high"
And fell out of bed with a jolt.

> Olive Guidera
> Ruthin, Clwyd

A Radio Wales listener from Holt
Didn't know a young mare from a colt
At the 'Horse of the Year'
His 'tranny' rang clear
And caused all the entries to bolt.

> Charles Latham
> Pwllheli, Gwynedd

A Radio Wales listener from Holt
Found himself in a state of revolt
When his income tax came
Said "It's always the same
It gives me one heck of a jolt."

> Kenvyn Davies
> Bridgend, Mid Glam.

A Radio Wales listener from Holt
From his crossbow once fired a bolt
Mike Flynn—he was shot
Alun Williams was not
'Cos he'd fled down the road like a colt.

> Elaine Gilbert
> Garnswllt, Ammanford, Dyfed

THERE WAS A YOUNG HAMSTER FROM NEATH

There was a young hamster from Neath
Who met a dear friend on the heath
He stood on his toes
And sniffed at her nose
Then nibbled her ears with his teeth.

> Ben E. Francis
> Pontlottyn, Bargoed, Mid Glam.

There was a young hampster from Neath
Who faintly resembled Ted Heath
Not its eyes or its nose
So I only suppose
It was something to do with its teeth.

> Kath Reed
> Middlezoy, Bridgwater, Somerset

There was a young hamster from Neath
Who fell for a parrot from Reith
The result of the match
An incredible batch
All feathers and fur and buck teeth.

> Mary Brunton
> Beeston, Nottingham

There was a young hampster from Neath
Had a habit of grinding his teeth
So a dentist he sought
When there wore down to nought
Now he's 'falsies' above and beneath.

> A. Windsor
> Cardiff, South Glam.

AT A NEW YEAR'S EVE PARTY IN NEATH

At a New Year's Eve party in Neath
A Scotsman who dropped his false teeth
In five feet of snow
Said "How can I go
Back to Leith with my teeth under Neath".

> John Halstead
> Caernarfon, Gwynedd

At a New Year's Eve party in Neath
I met a strange fellow called Keith
Who was drinking his beer
On his head, through his ear
And whistling 'Auld Lang Syne' through his teeth.

> Carolyn Wright
> Tyn-y-gongl, Gwynedd

At a New Year's Eve party in Neath
Was a brawny prop forward from Leith
Who started a fight
Which lasted all night
And went home minus sporran and teeth.

> Harry Hartill
> Rhydyfelin, Pontypridd, Mid Glam.

At a New Year's Eve party in Neath
Aunt Mabel mislaid her false teeth
So she rang 999
On the new party line
Enquiring 'Ith that the poleeth?"

> Alan Badmington
> Abergavenny, Gwent

A COMIC FROM CORNWALL CALLED HUGH

A comic from Cornwall called Hugh
Whose morals were straight-laced and true
Told Jokes that were clean
With no meanings obscene
Now he's part of the local dole queue.

> Tom Adams Jones
> Wrexham

A comic from Cornwall called Hugh
Each night played to more than a few
It wasn't Hugh's jokes
That brought in the folks
But his pretty young partner named Pru.

> Jean Oriel
> Mountain Ash, Mid Glam.

A comic from Cornwall called Hugh
Emigrated to Denmark from Looe
His nightclub routine
Was rather obscene
Now he's billed as the new 'Danish Blue'.

> Alan Badmington
> Abergavenny, Gwent

A comic from Cornwall called Hugh
Tried sweeping his chimney and flue
Said his wife, in a rage
"Hurry back to the stage
Or besides being black, you'll be blue".

> C. Tapp
> Gresford, Wrexham, Clwyd

A CLEVER OLD CLEANER FROM CLWYD

A clever old cleaner from Clwyd
Progressed through the Gorsedd to Druid
But his verses got worse
On account of his curse
An addiction to spirituous fluid.

> Vera Davies
> Cardiff, South Glam.

A clever old cleaner from Clwyd
Used to sunbathe at the home in the nwyd
But her husband Bill said
"Put a hat on your head
Or the neighbours will think you wost rwyd".

> George Lewis
> Claines, Worcester

A clever old cleaner from Clwyd
Invented a new cleansing fluid
But she mixed it too strong
It went off like a bomb
R.I.P. clever clear—you blew it.

> Vida Payne
> Llanishen, Cardiff, South Glam.

A clever old cleaner from Clwyd
Told jokes that were terribly lewd
They gave her the sack
But soon she was back
Having washed out her mouth with some fluid.

> Heather Davies
> Ruddlan, Clwyd

A HOLYHEAD BUTCHER NAMED FRED

A Holyhead butcher named Fred
To a lady once sold a sheep's head
Much to her surprise
He'd left in the eyes
'It will see you through Easter" he said.

> George Lewis
> Claines, Worcs.

A Holyhead butcher named Fred
When using a knife often bled
So ham-fisted was he
That he cut off his knee
But his wife stitched it on with some thread.

> Coral Courtney
> Llanelli, Dyfed

A Holyhead butcher named Fred
One night took his hatchet to bed
Amidst his deep dreaming
His wife started screaming
The reason, he'd chopped off her head.

> G. M. Hooper
> Pwll, Llanelli, Dyfed

A Holyhead butcher named Fred
Bought a racehorse, a pure thoroughbred
It went through its paces
But lost all its races
So he sold it as mincemeat instead.

> Viv Dann
> West Cross, Swansea, West Glam.

A CONSTABLE FROM CONNAH'S QUAY

A constable from Connah's Quay
Has a shocking vocabulary
Seems all that he knows
Are three quick 'Ello's'
And "You must accompany me".

> Alan Badmington
> Abergavenny, Gwent

A constable from Connah's Quay
With his butty went out on a spree
After whisky and wine
They were both feeling fine
Now they're spending the night in Cell 3.

> Glyn Prosser
> Sketty, Swansea, West Glam.

A constable from Connah's Quay
Fell in love with a lady P.C.
He took her to luncheon
But sat on his truncheon
Which filled all his rivals with glee.

> W. J. Delve
> West Cross, Swansea, West Glam.

A constable from Connah's Quay
Once arrested a drunk in a tree
But the drunk wasn't fussed
And he claimed it unjust
'Cos Special Branch he's with, you see.

> Ella Green
> Berkhamsted, Herts.

A FAT FATHER CHRISTMAS FROM FAIRBOURNE

A fat Father Christmas from Fairbourne
With reindeer and sledge soon got airborne
But when kicked by a hoof
He fell off the roof
So the rest of his Christmas was chairborne.

> A. Jenner
> Llantwit Major, South Glam.

A fat Father Christmas from Fairbourne
Was from Rudolph the Red Reindeer's lair borne
He hadn't a sled
So he used a large bed
And instead of a bell used an air horn.

> O. Williams
> Haverfordwest, Dyfed

A fat Father Christmas from Fairbourne
Last year was inclined to be swear prone
When stuck up a flue
He turned the air blue
And dropped down with beard and hair torn.

> John Adams,
> Caerleon, Newport, Gwent

A fat Father Christmas from Fairbourne
Had a terrible job getting airborne
Said Blitzen to Donna
"Next year I'm sure gonna
Make sure he diets to the barebone".

> Betty Fowles
> Port Talbot, West Glam.

A FLIER WHO FLEW OUT OF FAIRWOOD

A flyer who flew out of Fairwood
Had hopes that the thermals near there would
Give uplift and power
For a circuit round Gower
In a glider he'd made out of spare wood.

> Vera Davies
> Cardiff, South Glam.

A flyer who flew out of Fairwood
Said that just for a joke and a dare, would
Fly off to the stars
But his wig caught on Mars
Now he looks like a man with no hair should.

> Margaret Lusty
> Newport, Gwent

A flyer who flew out of Fairwood
Whose name was McDonald McHarewood
Went into the air
Upside down, for a dare
And behaved as a chap without care would.

> Glyn Prosser
> Sketty, Swansea, West Glam.

A flier who flew out of Fairwood
Said "You'd think people living round there would
Come out to admire
Such an ace of a flier
Red Baron, himself, would say 'Sehr gut' ".

> Ella Green
> Berkhamsted, Herts.

A BUSY YOUNG BARBER FROM SHOTTON

A busy young barber from Shotton
Nicked his customers' chins something rotten
He once made a slip
Gashed a man on the lip
Then he sewed it up neatly with cotton.

> Irene Mason
> Barry, South Glam.

A busy young barber from Shotton
Said "Hair style today is just rotten
So low has it sunk
They're all asking for punk
And 'short back and sides' is forgotten".

> Charles Latham
> Pwllheli, Gwynedd

A busy young barber from Shotton
Wore overalls made out of cotton
His meanness was such
That he wore them too much
Before very long they were rotten.

> Thelma Harding
> Cardiff, South Glam.

A busy young barber from Shotton
Still follows an art long forgotten
"Though 'short back and sides'
Is my best", he confides
"Most people say 'No leave the lot on' ".

> Nan Davies
> Menai Bridge, Anglesey, Gwynedd

A FRENCHMAN WHO SOLD FROZEN FOOD

A Frenchman who sold frozen food
Had a marketing system quite crude
On his bike he would ride
A small ice-box, each side
From which snails and frogs legs would protrude.

> Joan Salisbury
> Southport, Merseyside

A Frenchman who sold frozen food
To his clients was frequently rude
The silly old geezer
Would sit in a freezer
Whenever he got in a mood.

> Jean Oriel
> Mountain Ash, Mid Glam.

A Frenchman who sold frozen food
Said "My English is wrongly construed
I get my Oui Oui's
Confused with my peas
My customers think I am rude".

> Alan Badmington
> Abergavenny, Gwent

A Frenchman who sold frozen food
Kept chicken and had a nice brood
He hoped they would lay
When they grew up one day
But instead they just cock-a-doodle dooed.

> Ken Davies
> Brecon, Powys

A BEARDED YOUNG BUTCHER FROM RYE

A bearded young butcher from Rye
Was seen with a tear in his eye
He said, all aquiver
'Midst kidneys and liver
"I've just minced my flaming new tie".

E. J. Jones
Pentre, Chirk, Nr. Wrexham, Clwyd

A bearded young butcher from Rye
A lovely fair maid did espy
This delectable miss
With a passionate kiss
Ignited his facial fungi.

Mac Mason
Penllergaer, Swansea, West Glam.

A bearded young butcher from Rye
Decided to make shepherd's pie
There was only one snag
Though he'd spuds in the bag
Nice shepherds are hard to come by.

Marjorie Jones
Cardiff, South Glam.

A bearded young butcher from Rye
Emitted a blood-curdling cry
For while making mince
He started to wince
His beard had caught—my-oh-my!

Dennis J. Francis
Manselton, Swansea, West Glam.

A MOTORWAY BOUGHT ON H.P.

A motorway bought on H.P.
Conjures up some wild dreams, you'll agree
Imagine Town Hall
Announcing to all
"After 10 years you travel tax free".

> Betty Fowles
> Baglan Moor, Port Talbot, West Glam.

A motorway bought on H.P.
Was seized by the loan company
When I looked on the map
There it was—Watford Gap
The payments weren't kept up you see.

> Audrey Kenny
> Grangetown, Cardiff, South Glam.

A motorway bought on H.P.
Is so much a week, we agree
But with all the inflation
And the state of the nation
We won't pay by 2003.

> Betty Eardley
> Coedpoeth, Nr. Wrexham, Clwyd

A motorway bought on H.P.
Ran from Criccieth to Bangor-on-Dee
A policeman cried "Halt
There's a payment default
So travel via Llanfair P.G."

> Alan Thompson
> Colwyn Bay, Clwyd

AN ABSENT-MINDED PROFESSOR FROM KEELE

An absent-minded professor from Keele
Put his bike out of gear to free-wheel
Then forgetting of course
He was on a steel horse
Tried to tackle a hedge like John Peel.

> Halina Day
> Cardiff, South Glam.

An absent-minded professor from Keele
Was invited to lecture on steel
But he took the wrong notes
And spoke on wild goats
Causing laughter and many a squeal.

> Ben Barker
> Llanelli, Dyfed

An absent-minded professor from Keele
Went to fish with a new rod and reel
But what a to-do
When he fished up a shoe
And sat down to fried sole and 'eel.

> Betty Jones
> Pembroke Dock, Dyfed

An absent-minded professor from Keele
Was not known as one who would steal
But he once left a pub
Where he'd been for some grub
Forgetting to pay for his meal.

> Glyn Prosser
> Sketty, Swansea, West Glam.

117

A PONTYPRIDD SINGER CALLED JONES

A Pontypridd singer called Jones
Had a voice of peculiar tones
When he reached a top note
His vibrating throat
Would damage a few microphones.

> G. J. Prosser
> Sketty, Swansea, West Glam.

A Pontypridd singer called Jones
While swinging on stage, broke some bones
Then he went down with gout
And his front teeth fell out
So now he won't sing, he just moans.

> Julie Dobbins
> Gorseinon, Swansea, West Glam.

A Pontypridd singer called Jones
Has a wife who continually moans
"Stop shaking your hip
You give me the pip
And your trousers keep splitting", she groans

> June Harris
> Beaumaris, Anglesey

A Pontypridd singer called Jones
Made a cult of gyrating his bones
And even the sheep
Were unable to sleep
When the valleys rang out to his tones.

> Charles Latham
> Pwllheli, Gwynedd

A MAGISTRATE FROM MOUNTAIN ASH

A magistrate from Mountain Ash
Grew a rather ridiculous moustache
When prisoners poked fun
He sentenced each one
To forty nine strokes of the lash.

> Anne Treharne
> Tonyrefail, Mid Glam.

A magistrate from Mountain Ash
Reached the courtroom in rather a dash
Much to his distress
He'd forgotten to dress
Now he's known to the ushers as 'Flash'.

> Alan Badmington
> Abergavenny, Gwent

A magistrate from Mountain Ash
Told a crook (as he twirled his moustache)
"I'll uphold your appeal
If you make a fair deal
Just say where you've hidden the cash".

> J. L. Edwards
> Gobowen, Oswestry, Shropshire

A magistrate from Mountain Ash
Grew so fat—'cause he ate too much mash
His robes would not fit
And his trousers, he split
Worse—he fell off the Bench with a crash.

> Hilda Jones
> Penycae, Wrexham, Clwyd

A MASTER MECHANIC FROM MOLD

A master mechanic from Mold
All the girls in his arms would enfold
But each time he would spoil
Their clean dresses, with oil
Leaving clues to the parts he did hold.

> Ken Waterman
> Bridgend, Mid Glam.

A master mechanic from Mold
Had a secret that now has been told
His gift to Diana
A left-handed spanner
That was moulded in solid Welsh gold.

> Teifion James
> Aberporth, Dyfed

A master mechanic from Mold
Owned a garage where used cars were sold
His name was quite shocking
For speedometer clocking
Now he's serving six months, so I'm told.

> Alan Badmington
> Abergavenny, Gwent

A master mechanic from Mold
Liked to tinker with cars that were old
He would work day and night
To make sure they were right
And was sad when they had to be sold.

> Barbara Cotton
> Wrexham, Clwyd

A MAD MAGICIAN FROM MUMBLES

A mad magician from Mumbles
Saws people in half, but he fumbles
Since he goes quite insane
If one dares to complain
Though folk are 'cut up', no one grumbles.

> Ella Green
> Berkhamsted, Herts.

A mad magician from Mumbles
Did a trick with some bees, quite large bumbles
He made them appear
From inside his ear
But they stung him and brought forth loud grumbles.

> Jean Oriel
> Mountain Ash

A mad magician from Mumbles
Had a wife, full of moans, groans and grumbles
So one day for a laugh
He sawed her in half
When she tries to stand up now—she tumbles.

> Hilda Jones
> Penycae, Wrexham, Clwyd

A mad magician from Mumbles
Whose tummy was subject to rumbles
Wrote many fine tunes
To amuse other loons
On the themes of his interior grumbles.

> Doreen Hill
> Cullompton, Devon

A PRETTY YOUNG LADY CALLED JENNY

A pretty young lady named Jenny
Once needed to spend a quick penny
But the town she was at
Had no building like that
So she drove like the wind to Ewenny.

> Natalie Webb
> Flint, Clwyd

A pretty young lady named Jenny
Was courting a fellow named Lenny
They went for a walk
And had no time to talk
But their kisses and cuddles were many.

> V. Nicholas,
> Pendine, Carmarthen, Dyfed

A pretty young lady named Jenny
Ate cream cakes and buns—much too many
She doubled in size
But that wasn't wise
No weighing scale now takes her penny.

> Coral Courtney
> Llanelli, Dyfed

A pretty young lady named Jenny
Of boyfriends I think she had many
Why didn't she wed?
"Not likely" she said
"If I did that, I wouldn't have any".

> Charles Latham,
> Pwllheli, Gwynedd

VALENTINE LIMERICKS

"On St. Valentine's Day" said young Rose
"My boy-friend knelt down to propose
I was all of a flutter
But all he could mutter
Was, 'I can see right up your nose' ".

> Dennis Collins
> Upton, Wirrall

A gent who's 103
Sends valentine cards constantly
As I'm 97
I should be in heaven
But mum says he's too old for me.

> Alan Badmington
> Abergavenny, Gwent

On Valentine's Day he forgot
Forgiven? oh no, he was not
For not sending a card
She hit him with lard
But it burned, 'cos the chip pan was hot.

> Jane Shearer Parry
> Nannerch, Mold, Clwyd

In the Muppets' New Year of the Frog
Old Kermit, while sat on a log
To Miss Piggy did say
"As it's Valentine's Day
I thought we might go the whole hog".

> Jim Quick
> Honiton, Devon

A SPACEMAN WHO LANDED FROM MARS

A spaceman who landed from Mars
At the local called in for some jars
He said "Landlord dear
I'm just here for the beer
And to sample your tasty Mars Bars".

> M. Miles
> Goodwick, Dyfed

A spaceman who landed from Mars
Developed a passion for cars
He first took a Maxi
And then stole a taxi
And so ended up behind bars.

> Joye Lafford
> Griffithstown, Pontypool, Gwent

A spaceman who landed from Mars
Espied one of Earth's bubble cars
Without losing face
Explained that they place
Not Martians but goldfish in jars.

> Geraint Jenkins
> Ystradgynlais, Swansea

A spaceman who landed from Mars
Got strange looks in Swansea pub bars
'Cos he copied the vocals
Of Welsh speaking locals
And ordered two small bore da's.

> Sandra Sinclair
> Pembroke, Dyfed

A LLANDRINDOD VICAR SAID "MY"

A Llandrindod Vicar said "My
It's so cold that my font has gone dry
All icy and glistening
I can't do the christening
Perhaps you'll come back in July".

> Eirwen Rogers
> Merthyr Tydfil, Mid Glam.

A Llandrindod vicar said "My
This vestry looks like a pigsty
The choirboys, though charming
Have habits alarming
And the choirmaster smells rather high".

> Brian Burge
> Llandudno Junction, Gwynedd

A Llandrindod vicar said "My
Church figures have gone up sky high
It's not due to me
But my daughter, you see
Whose dresses show far too much thigh".

> Jean Oriel
> Mountain Ash, Mid Glam.

A Llandrindod vicar said "My
This collar's so tight I could die
Whilst chanting, I'm ranting
And puffing and panting
Next week, I will wear a bow-tie".

> Marlene Kerr
> Rhydlewis, Llandyssul, Dyfed

129

A MARKET INSPECTOR FROM FLINT

A market inspector from Flint
Was born with a terrible squint
Whilst dancing with Betty
His eyes were on Lettie
Which caused her to blush a bright pink.

> Gwenfyl Bennett
> St. David's, Dyfed

A market inspector from Flint
Would sneeze when in contact with mint
As he had to use tissues
To avoid his atishoos
The greengrocers' stalls made him skint.

> Thelma Harding
> Cardiff, South Glam.

A market inspector from Flint
Put amorous poems in print
They read them with glee
From Neath to Cwmdu
And the royalties made him a mint.

> Elaine Gilbert
> Garnswllt, Ammanford, Dyfed

A market inspector from Flint
Who everyone reckoned was skint
Concealed all his loot
In the heel of his boot
The crafty old boy's worth a mint.

> Ellen Monk
> Swansea, West Glam.

AN M.P. WHO VISITED MUMBLES

An M.P. who visited Mumbles
Had a wife with abdominal rumbles
She said "Now my dear
The noises you hear
Are due to your amorous fumbles".

> Raymond Stobbard
> Rhuddlan, Clwyd

An M.P. who visited Mumbles
Met a man who kept bees, mostly bumbles
He said "When it's sunny
I gets lots of honey
But when we have rainfall, I grumbles".

> Dave Hill,
> Whitchurch, Bristol

An M.P. who visited Mumbles
Found the voters had plenty of grumbles
One threw a bad egg
Then a dog bit his leg
Now he pongs and he frequently stumbles.

> W. J. Delce
> West Cross, Swansea, West Glam.

An M.P. who visited Mumbles
Took part in the games and the tumbles
Then feeling quite proud
He said to the crowd
"Makes a change from brick-bats and grumbles".

> Audrey Guy
> Crofty, Swansea, West Glam.

A SLOPPY OLD SPEAKER NAMED SPOONER

A sloppy old speaker named Spooner
Got wed to a fat girl called Oona
We're not telling lies
But so big was her size
That to catch her, he had to harpoon her.

> Ben Barker
> Llanelli, Dyfed

A sloppy old speaker named Spooner
Was a guest at a dinner in Poona
He dribbled—I'm blowed
'Til his soup overflowed
Causing flooding in Tristan Da Cunha.

> R. C. H. Gravelle
> Killay, Swansea, West Glam.

A sloppy old speaker named Spooner
Who fancied himself as a crooner
Tried to emulate Bing
But just could not sing
Like pianos, he needed a tuner.

> J. Edwards
> Gobowen, Oswestry, Shropshire

A sloppy old speaker named Spooner
Sailed to the South Seas in a schooner
Where for his mixed words
He's loved by the birds
And lives like a young honeymooner.

> Bill Hardy
> Evington, Leicester

A YOUNG DEEP-SEA DIVER FROM DALLAS

A young deep-sea diver from Dallas
Was invited to tea at the Palace
When he rudely refused
The Queen—not amused
Cried "Off with his head", like in 'Alice'!

> Hilda Jones
> Penycae, Wrexham

A young deep-sea diver from Dallas
Although he's not usually callous
Saw J.R.'s bunch on a yacht
So he scuttled the lot
And got an M.C. from the palace.

> Ella Green
> Berkhamsted, Herts.

A young deep-sea diver from Dallas
Has a voice like Maria La Callas
It wasn't a lark
But a fast moving shark
Why he's no longer Alan but Alice.

> Charles Latham
> Pwllheli, Gwynedd

A young deep-sea diver from Dallas
Shot J.R. with forethought and malice
The world was delighted
And he was soon knighted
On a visit to Buckingham Palace.

> Hazel Hill
> Iver Heath, Bucks.

A MARKET STALL HOLDER FROM GOWER

A market stall-holder from Gower
Was heard to proclaim of his flour
"It's truly amazing
Not only self-raising
But'll put any man in your power".

> Jenny Packer
> Little Leigh, Northwich, Cheshire

A market stall-holder from Gower
Once fell from a very tall tower
He landed somehow
On a Hereford cow
Now she gives milk that's terribly sour.

> Jon Tovey,
> Ilminster, Somerset

A market stall-holder from Gower
Was gifted with hypnotic power
When folk came to buy
He would soon catch their eye
And his till would be full in an hour.

> Coral Courtney
> Llanelli, Dyfed

A market stall-holder from Gower
To Chester he went, in an hour
When asked how he'd sped
Explained "It's the bread
Which gives everyone flour power".

> V. Homer
> Connah's Quay, Deeside, Clwyd

WHILE ROUND AT THE VICAR'S FOR TEA

While round at the vicar's for tea
I knelt down to pray on one knee
He said, with a frown
"Put the other leg down
And offer a quick one for me".

> Huw Cogbill
> Llanharan, Mid Glam.

While round at the vicar's for tea
A choirboy tucked in with glee
He stuffed himself 'til
He'd had more than his fill
Then he was as sick as could be.

> Keith Coles
> Tondu, Bridgend, Mid Glam.

While round at the vicar's for tea
Young Mark said to his brother Lee
"They can keep loaves and fishes
And those biblical dishes
It's jelly and custard for me".

> Alan Badmington
> Abergavenny, Gwent

While round at the vicar's for tea
The bishop said "I must agree
The 'Star' and the 'Sun'
Are always great fun
But I never look at Page Three".

> Jeff Williams
> Bargoed, Mid Glam.

136

A LICENSEE FROM LITTLE MILL

A licensee from Little Mill
Got mad with a customer Will
Who said "Keep your beer
It's flat and too dear
And your pies need a pneumatic drill".

> W. J. Delve
> West Cross, Swansea, West Glam.

A licensee from Little Mill
Affectionately known as 'Our Lil'
Refused to serve drunks
Mods, skinheads or punks
But the good guys could drink to their fill.

> Jack Jenkins
> Monkswood, Usk, Gwent

A licensee from Little Mill
Never gives his beer glasses a swill
Just imagine those dregs
Of stale cider and kegs
The thought of it makes one quite ill.

> Alan Badmington
> Abergavenny, Gwent

A licensee from Little Mill
Is known as Security Bill
In the bar he's got Anna
In the lounge a large scanner
And a dirty great lock on the till.

> Ronnie Charles
> Ebbw Vale, Gwent

137

A BUSKER WHO BASKED IN THE SUN

A busker who basked in the sun
Said "Goodness, oh what have I done
My didgeree doo
Has melted in two
And my show still has two weeks to run.

> Susan Walker
> Cheltenham, Glos.

A busker who basked in the sun
Played a tune in the nude, just for fun
As he lay there bare chested
He was promptly arrested
But escaped and is now on the run.

> Alan Badmington
> Abergavenny, Gwent

A busker who basked in the sun
Asked a female if he looked well done
"I'll tell you" she said
"If you'll stand on your head
And play that tune, 'Run Rabbit Run' ".

> Jean Griffiths
> Mountain Ash, Mid Glam.

A busker who basked in the sun
Had forgotten before he'd begun
To shade his guitar
Which got too hot, by far
And the strings snapped, like shots from a gun.

> Ella Green
> Berkhamsted, Herts.

A BUSY YOUNG MIDWIFE FROM YORK

A busy young midwife from York
Said "It's action—I've no time to talk
My bag, I've mislaid
And I can't find a spade
So I'll manage with small knife and fork".

> George Lewis
> Claines, Worcs.

A busy young midwife from York
To a Young Farmers' Group gave a talk
She heard someone mutter
"Please sample our butter
You'll soon tell the difference from Stork".

> Alan Badmington
> Abergavenny, Gwent

A busy young midwife from York
Maintained a 'hot line' to the stork
In all matters medical
Especially obstetrical
She's a gynaecological hawk.

> Tom Adams Jones
> Wrexham, Clwyd

A busy young midwife from York
Just couldn't keep up with the stork
She said "Mrs. Tate
So sorry I'm late
But he flies and I have to walk".

> Frank Jones
> Llangranog, Llandysul, Dyfed

A SILLY OLD SALESMAN FROM STOKE

A silly old salesman from Stoke
Overnight put his false teeth to soak
By the very next day
They had melted away
And his chin touched his nose when he spoke.

> Hilda Jones
> Penycae, Wrexham

A silly old salesman from Stoke
Each morning, in bed, when he woke
Would eat egg on toast
As he read through his post
So his letters got covered in yolk.

> Ella Green
> Berkhamsted, Herts.

A silly old salesman from Stoke
Drove around in an old Mini Moke
Selling bloomers and knickers
Rear car window stickers
And even the odd sack of coke.

> Joan Cole
> Tenby Dyfed

A silly old salesman from Stoke
Was a terrible wag of a bloke
He sold leaking pots
To incontinent Scots
That was his idea of a joke.

> Garnet and Rene Phillips
> Pembrey, Burry Port, Dyfed

AN UNDERSIZED PLUMBER FROM POOLE

A undersized plumber from Poole
Said "My workmates now all ridicule
The boss wanted a wrench
But I thought he said 'wench'
And I came back with Bridget O'Toole".

> M. Phillips
> Llandaff North, Cardiff, South Glam.

An undersized plumber from Poole
Deliberately used the wrong tool
He left a big gap
In the bar counter tap
So beer would flow free—he's no fool.

> Halina Day
> Cardiff, South Glam.

An undersized plumber from Poole
Said "Cor, I don't half feel a fool
'Cos I can't reach the taps
When I'm wearing my daps
So I have to climb up on a stool".

> Jean Oriel
> Mountain Ash, Mid Glam.

An undersized plumber from Poole
At lunch-time would frequently drool
While his mates enjoyed ham,
Pork, chicken or lamb
He had to endure his Ma's gruel.

> Yvonne Courtney
> Llanelli, Dyfed

IN THE CHINESE NEW YEAR OF THE DOG

In the Chinese New Year of the Dog
Said Dai Jones, who's a bit of a hog
"They may eat Pot Noodles
But surely not poodles
Does France have a Year of the Frog?"

> S. C. Baird
> Penarth, South Glam.

In the Chinese New Year of the Dog
A girl kissed a boy in the fog
But it made the lass wince
When she found that her Prince
Was transferred to a ruddy great frog.

> George Lewis
> Claines, Worcs.

In the Chinese New Year of the Dog
The customers looked all agog
While the town Take-Away
Celebrated the day
With free bamboo shoots and some grog.

> Ann Marling
> Llanharan, Mid Glam.

In the Chinese New Year of the Dog
Wing Ling took his Peke for a jog
While crossing the park
It started to bark
Then watered its favourite log.

> Alan Badmington
> Abergavenny, Gwent

A CHOIRBOY FROM RHOS-UPON-SEA

A choirboy from Rhos-upon-Sea
Arrived late for practice—Ah me!
The vicar was mad
So punishing the lad
By making him late home for tea.

> R. Parker
> North Cheam, Surrey

A choirboy from Rhos-upon-Sea
Always sings the main verse in low key
But to render descants
He wears tighter pants
Or else he won't manage top 'C'.

> Alan Badmington
> Abergavenny, Gwent

A choirboy from Rhos-upon-Sea
Was singing while having his tea
When a half-swallowed prune
Put a stop to his tune
To the joy of his own family.

> Keith Coles
> Tondu, Bridgend, Mid Glam.

A choirboy from Rhos-upon-Sea
Looked an angel to you or to me
But under his ruff
He'd a packet of snuff
And a catapult tied to his knee.

> Geraldine Richards
> Ffordd Dyfed, Tywyn, Gwynedd

FOUR HITCH-HIKERS EN ROUTE TO SPAIN

Four hitch-hikers en route to Spain
Tried hard for a lift but in vain
In spite of their thumbing
No lift was forthcoming
So it's two weeks in Scunthorpe again.

> W. J. Delve
> West Cross, Swansea, West Glam.

Four hitch-hikers en route to Spain
Two shapely and pretty, two plain
The ones with the gifts
Got all of the lifts
The other two boarded a train.

> Ella Green
> Berkhamsted, Berks.

Four hitch-hikers en route to Spain
In the mountains encountered no rain
They later found out
There wasn't a drought
Just, it mainly falls on the plain.

> Alan Badmington
> Abergavenny, Gwent

Four hitch-hikers en route to Spain
Two Scots, one Swede and a Dane
Just couldn't agree
On land, air or sea
So they travelled by underground train.

> Marguerite Prisk
> Penarth, South Glam.

A WONDERFUL WIZARD FROM WICK

A wonderful wizard from Wick
On a friend, with his spells, played a trick
He changed the man's watch
To a bottle of Scotch
So instead of 'tick-tock' it went 'hic'.

> Ella Green
> Berkhamsted, Herts.

A wonderful wizard from Wick
Swallows swords, it's his favourite trick
One day it mis-fired
And now he's retired
Without tonsils, he's feeling quite sick.

> Mac Mason
> Penllergaer, Swansea, West Glam.

A wonderful wizard from Wick
With cards, was amazingly slick
His prestidigitation
Would cause a sensation—
His WHAT? (Well it means he was quick.)

> Mary Brunton
> Beeston, Nottingham

A wonderful wizard from Wick
Changed Stewart to Flynn in a tick
Though inclined to confuse
Whoever you choose
Gives a programme that's racey and slick.

> Jon Tovey
> Ilminster, Somerset

A BONNY WEE LASS FROM DUNDEE

A bonny wee lass from Dundee
Got wed to a Scot named McPhee
It caused quite a smile
When they walked down the aisle
'Cos right up his kilt you could see.

> George Lewis
> Claines, Worcs.

A bonny wee lass from Dundee
Had a handsome young man round to tea
He said "Now my dear
You've nothing to fear
It's your dumplings I'm after, not thee".

> W. J. Delve
> West Cross, Swansea, West Glam.

A bonny wee lass from Dundee
Once married a man from Southsea
They had haggis each day
Much to hubby's dismay
Now he prays for a Devonshire tea.

> Lily Kaye
> Dinas Powis, South Glam.

A bonny wee lass from Dundee
Drank a bottle of whisky for tea
All the neighbours were shocked
As she reeled and she rocked
With one knicker leg over her knee.

> Hilda Jones
> Penycae, Wrexham

A GYMNAST WHO TRAINED IN THE GYM

A gymnast who trained in the gym
Was advised, by his team mates, to slim
Now he's thinner by far
Than a parallel bar
And instead of the beam, they use him.

Ella Green
Berkhamsted, Herts.

A gymnast who trained in the gym
Was known as 'Superman Jim'
In physique he was strong
But in height—ten foot long
Too much practice had stretched every limb.

Coral Courtney
Llanelli, Dyfed

A gymnast who trained in the gym
Worked daily to stay sleek and slim
Though his floor work was great
The food that he ate
Made his gymnastics future look grim.

Eirwen Rogers
Merthyr Tydfil, Mid Glam.

A gymnast who trained in the gym
Each day, full of vigour and vim
Did one hand-stand too much
Now he walks with a crutch
And has bandages on every limb.

Hilda Jones
Penycae, Wrexham

A MERRY OLD DOCTOR FROM PYLE

A merry old doctor from Pyle
Told a health conscious man—"Wait awhile
Don't jog all your life
Try taking a wife
'Cause a Mrs is good as a mile".

Ella Green
Berkhamsted, Herts.

A merry old doctor from Pyle
Would watch people die—with a smile
Before they fell ill
He'd be named in their will
No wonder he lives in such style.

Sam Evans
Middleton, Oswestry, Shropshire

A merry old doctor from Pyle
Possessed a sure treatment for bile
The patients—though moaning
Complaining and groaning
Were fed to a large crocodile.

C. Harrison
Capel Ifan, Nr. Newcastle Emlyn, Dyfed

A merry old doctor from Pyle
Would treat female patients with style
As the ladies came in
He would bring out the gin
And they always left with a smile.

Ted Callaghan
Reynoldston, Swansea, West Glam.

A LADY FROM HAVERFORDWEST

A lady from Haverfordwest
Just loves showing off her bare chest
But it's not a scandal
For little Miss Randall
Is only six months—had you guessed?

> Jean Oriel
> Mountain Ash, Mid Glam.

A lady from Haverfordwest
Discarded her warm winter vest
She contracted 'flu'
Pneumonia too
Now lies in a Chapel of Rest.

> D. N. Francis
> Pontardulais, Swansea, West Glam.

A lady from Haverfordwest
Had three curly hairs on her chest
She said "Should I shave 'em
Or permanent wave 'em
I don't know what to do for the best."

> John Williams
> Hverfordwest, Dyfed

A lady from Haverfordwest
After failing three times with her test
Said "I'll still have to hike
Or else buy a bike
And pedal to work like the rest".

> Glyn Prosser
> Sketty, Swansea, West Glam.

A LADY WHO JUMPED ON HER SCALES

A lady who jumped on her scales
Saw her weight and went right off the rails
To help with her slimming
She tried channel swimming
But was shot by some men hunting whales.

> W. J. Delve
> West Cross, Swansea, West Glam.

A lady who jumped on her scales
Ran away to a health farm in Wales
They fed her on leeks
For seven whole weeks
And made her play rugby in gales.

> Carolyn Wright
> Tynygongl, Gwynedd

A lady who jumped on her scales
Said "My diet has gone off the rails"
But later she found
That to lose the odd pound
One foot on the floor never fails.

> Jonathan Barry Ralstons
> Edgeware, Middlesex

A lady who jumped on her scales
Broke the spring and cried out with loud wails
Now she's weighed in a sack
Like the good nutty slack
At the coalyard alongside the rails.

> J. Wright
> Tynygongl, Gwynedd

A DOCTOR FROM LLANFAIR P.G.

A doctor from Llanfair P.G.
Was run in whilst out on a spree
The police sergeant cried
Where d'you live? He replied, "At
Llanfairpwllgwyngyllgogerychwyrndrobwllantysyliogogogoch"
—He went free.

Alan Thompson
Rhos-on-Sea, Colwyn Bay, Clwyd

A doctor from Llanfair P.G.
Said to his dear wife Rose-Marie
"Just look what I've found
If I change this name round
I can call myself Llanfair's G.P."

O. Hughes
Pengorffwysfa, Llaneilian, Gwynedd

A doctor from Llanfair P.G.
Was stung on the nose by a bee
He ran for a plaster
But should have run faster
'Cos another one stung his left knee.

Christine Jones
Bangor, Gwynedd

A doctor from Llanfair P.G.
Prescribed a long swim in the sea
For Paddy's bad back
But he hadn't the knack
And went down like a stone—R.I.P.

J. R. Jones
Marchwiel, Wrexham

A PRESCRIPTION PRESCRIBER FROM PILL

A prescription prescriber from Pill
Kept a gaggle of geese on the hill
The grease from the goose
He put to good use
For injections, he used a blunt quill (Ouch!!).

> Marguerite Prisk
> Penarth, South Glam.

A prescription prescriber from Pill
Undertook he could cure any ill
His sublime panacea
Made all pains disappear
Except for the shock of his bill.

> Eric Robinson
> Whitchurch, Cardiff, South Glam.

A prescription prescriber from Pill
Took a generous sum from the till
With his pestle and mortar
And his boss's young daughter
He started a business in Rhyl.

> S. Burgis Parish
> Ealing, London W.5.

A prescription prescriber from Pill
Abused his medicinal skill
For a mere fifty pence
He would freely dispense
A potion intended to kill.

> Alan Badmington
> Abergavenny, Gwent

A NASTY YOUNG DENTIST FROM NEATH

A nasty young dentist from Neath
On his surgery door hung a wreath
Plus a notice which said
"Come in live—go out dead
I take blood with my Dracula teeth".

> Mai M. Roach
> Haverfordwest, Dyfed

A nasty young dentist from Neath
Looked quite like ex P.M. Ted Heath
So he posed as a Tory
Called his yacht 'Morning Glory'
Shook his shoulders and bared all his teeth.

> Jean Griffiths
> Mountain Ash, Mid Glam.

A nasty young dentist from Neath
Made his mother a set of false teeth
He lined them with gold
So that when she was cold
He'd have money to buy her a wreath.

> Jean Bray
> Radyr, Cardiff, South Glam.

A nasty young dentist from Neath
Gave notice and moved up to Leith
Of pulling and filling
Cementing and drilling
He was really fed up to his teeth.

> · Susan MacMillan
> Treorchy, Rhondda, Mid Glam.

A DASHING YOUNG PILOT FROM RHOOSE

A dashing young pilot from Rhoose
For compasses had little use
He set off to fly
To the island of Skye
But landed instead at Toulouse.

> Jessie Carr
> Menai Bridge, Anglesey, Gwynedd

A dashing young pilot from Rhoose
Built a plane that he called 'The Wild Goose'
He did spins, loops and glides
And charges £5 for rides
Which helped him to pay for the juice.

> Hilda Jones
> Penycae, Wrexham, Clwyd

A dashing young pilot from Rhoose
Said "Women are really the deuce
I crash landed in Rome
But when I 'phoned home
My wife said 'That's just your excuse' ".

> Ella Green
> Berkhamsted, Herts.

A dashing young pilot from Rhoose
Flew high on the back of a goose
As he sped through the air
He tried, with great care
To hijack a plane with a noose.

> F. Bremner
> Cardiff, South Glam.

THE STARLING PRESS LTD

PRINTERS, PUBLISHERS AND ADVERTISING CONTRACTORS

Registered Office
TREDEGAR STREET RISCA NEWPORT GWENT NP1 6YB

Member of the Newport Chamber of Trade

Publishers of
South Wales Authors & South Wales Books

Member of Independent Publishers Guild

Telephone Risca 612251 (STD 0633 612251)

GENERAL PRINTING
LETTERPRESS & LITHO

*For Industry and Commerce, Schools and Colleges,
Catalogues, Brochures, Books, Magazines, Schedules,
Leaflets, Letterheads, Programmes,
Order Pads, Directories, Colour Printing.*

BOOK PRINTING FOR PUBLISHERS

Catalogues about our books are
South Wales Books My Scene (1978)
(F E A Yates
South Wales Books Scene Two (1983)
(F E A Yates)